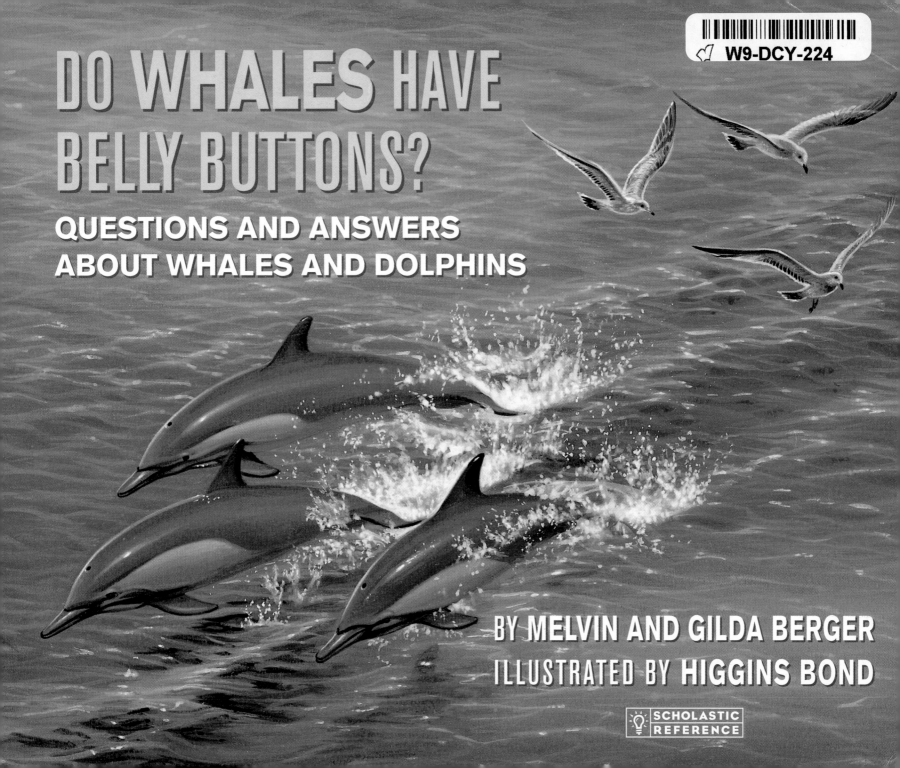

DO WHALES HAVE BELLY BUTTONS?

QUESTIONS AND ANSWERS ABOUT WHALES AND DOLPHINS

BY MELVIN AND GILDA BERGER

ILLUSTRATED BY HIGGINS BOND

SCHOLASTIC REFERENCE

Contents

KEY TO ABBREVIATIONS
cm = centimeter/centimetre
kg = kilogram
km = kilometer/kilometre
l = liter
m = meter/metre
t = tonne

Text copyright © 1999 by Melvin Berger and Gilda Berger
Illustration copyright © 1999 by Barbara Higgins Bond
All rights reserved. Published by Scholastic Inc.
SCHOLASTIC and associated logos are trademarks and/or registered trademarks of Scholastic Inc.

Library of Congress Cataloging-in-Publication Data
Berger, Melvin.
  Do whales have belly buttons? / Melvin & Gilda Berger:
  [illustrated by Barbara Higgins Bond].
  Summary: Provides answers to such questions about various species of whales and dolphins as "Do all whales have teeth?" , "How long do whales live?" , "Why do dolphins whistle?" , and "Can dolphins save humans?"
  ISBN   0-590-13088-9 (alk. paper)
  1. Whales—Miscellanea—Juvenile literature. [1. Whales—Miscellanea.
  2. Questions and answers.] I. Berger, Gilda. II. Bond, Barbara Higgins, ill. III. Title.
QL737.C4B64   1999   599.5—dc21   98-13430   CIP   AC

Book design by David Saylor and Nancy Sabato

10 9 8 7 6 5 4 3 2 1   9/9 0/0 01 02 03

Printed in the U.S.A.   08
First printing, February 1999

Expert readers: Robert Cummings and Lisa Mielke
Aquarium for Wildlife Conservation
Brooklyn, New York

To the Whale of a Team at Scholastic Reference

— M. AND G. BERGER

This book about the magnificent animals of the ocean is dedicated to the most magnificent person I know, my sister, Deborah Lynn Higgins

— HIGGINS BOND

Introduction

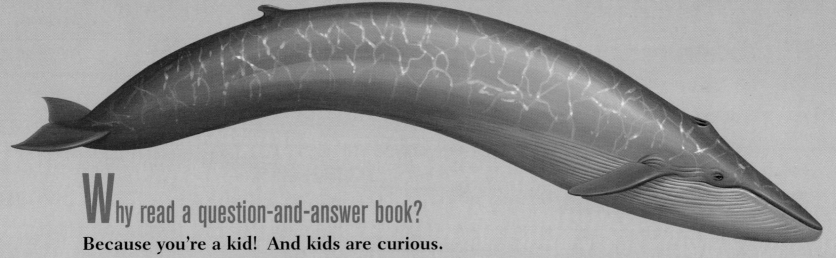

Why read a question-and-answer book?

Because you're a kid! And kids are curious.

It's natural—and important—to ask *questions* and look for *answers*.

This book answers many questions that you may have:

- How long can whales stay under water?
- How do whales keep in touch?
- Can dolphins save humans?
- Which whales have the longest migration?

Many of the answers will surprise and amaze you. We hope they'll tickle your imagination. Maybe they will lead you to ask *more questions* calling for *more answers*. That's what being curious is all about!

Melvin Berger   *Gilda Berger*

THE LIFE OF A WHALE

Do whales have belly buttons?

Yes. Whales have belly buttons, just like dogs and cats, lions and tigers, you and me. Like these other animals, a whale develops inside its mother's body. The unborn whale is connected to its mother by an umbilical cord. After birth, the umbilical cord snaps off. In time, the cord withers away. What's left is a belly button on the whale's underside.

Are whales mammals?

Yes. Mammals are animals that are born alive and feed on their mothers' milk. They breathe air and are warm-blooded, keeping the same body temperature no matter how cold or warm their surroundings. And all mammals have hair—even if it's only a few bristles like the whales.

Are fish mammals?

No. Fish hatch from eggs that females lay almost anywhere. In general, fish are cold-blooded. Their body temperature is about the same as the water in which they live. They breathe through gills, and most are covered with hard scales. Even the biggest sharks are fish—and of course, sharks don't have belly buttons.

Are whales the only mammals in the sea?

No. Whales belong to a group of sea-dwelling mammals that includes dolphins and porpoises. These animals are called cetaceans (sih-TAY-shuns). Cetaceans have the shape of fish and live in the water, but they are mammals.

Walruses, seals, and sea otters are also mammals that live in the sea. But they are not cetaceans. Nobody would mistake them for fish!

How many babies do whales have?

Usually only one baby at a time. Sometimes twins are born, but this is rare. A baby whale is called a calf.

Female whales, known as cows, carry their unborn young 9 to 18 months. Most cows give birth every 2 to 5 years.

How are calves born?

In water and usually tail first. This is different from most land mammals, which are born head first.

After birth, the calf rolls in the water like a barrel. Using her flippers and body, the mother sets the calf right side up. Then she pushes it to the surface for its first breath of air. Often other whales, called aunts, lend a flipper!

What does a calf eat?

Mother's milk—just like other mammals. It nurses by taking a nipple into its mouth. The nipple is tucked inside the cow's skin fold. The calf swallows a huge stream of milk that the cow squirts into its throat. The calf nurses for short lengths of time because the milk is very rich. Every so often, the calf surfaces for a quick breath of air.

The milk is said to taste like a mixture of fish, liver, milk of magnesia, and castor oil. But baby whales seem to like it. They gain as much as 200 pounds (90 kg) a day!

How long do calves nurse?

For 6 months to 2 years. It all depends on the kind of whale.

How do whales breathe?

Through nostrils, called blowholes. The blowholes are at the top of the head. This lets whales breathe even when most of their body is under the water.

Before taking a deep dive, called sounding, a whale fills its lungs with air. Underwater, it holds its breath. But sooner or later, it must come up to the surface for a breath of fresh air. But first—VOOM—it blasts out the stale air, called the blow, at a speed of about 300 miles (480 km) an hour!

What does the whale blow look like?

A puffy cloud. The air the whale breathes out is warm and moist. When it hits the colder outside air, it forms a cloud of tiny drops of water. It looks like your breath on a cold day.

Sometimes a whale blows just below the surface. Then the blow also sprays seawater with the escaping air. This blow looks like a fountain. A single blow can be as high as a three-story building!

Whale blows have different sizes and shapes. One kind is short and round, for example. Another is tall and narrow. Some people can tell one kind of a whale from another just by the look of its blow!

Do whales have bad breath?

Some say so. Sailors and people who work with whales tell us that the blow smells fishy. Perhaps the bad smell comes from the whales' diet and life in the sea.

One day you may go whale watching and get very close to a large whale when it blows. Then you can find out for yourself if whales have bad breath!

How long can whales stay under water?

From 20 minutes to 2 hours. Whale dives last far longer than human dives. Even the best human diver can stay under water only a few minutes without coming up for air.

Whale blood holds more oxygen than human blood. Also, taking several deep breaths before it dives adds extra oxygen to a whale's blood. During the dive, the whale draws on this stored-up supply of oxygen. When it's gone, the whale returns to the surface—and "thar she blows!"

Do whales have especially large lungs?

No. They just make good use of the lungs they do have. For example, when you breathe deeply you fill about one fourth of your lungs with air. But when whales breathe in, the air fills almost all of their lungs.

Also, whales use up the air in their lungs more slowly than you do. That's because a whale's heartbeat gets slower when it dives. A slow heartbeat helps stretch the supply of air.

Can whales drown?

Yes. Whales drown if water enters their blowholes. This happens when whales get sick, hurt, or tangled up in nets or lines under the sea. If a whale is unable to swim to the surface to breathe, it will die by drowning.

Why do whales sometimes get stuck on shore?

No one knows for sure. But whales sometimes swim onto a beach and get stranded there. A stranding of 20 or more whales at a time is called a mass stranding.

Stranded whales often live for several days on their own. If high tide sweeps water over the whale, it might drown. With kind treatment, whales may be kept alive longer and helped back into the sea.

Fin Whale

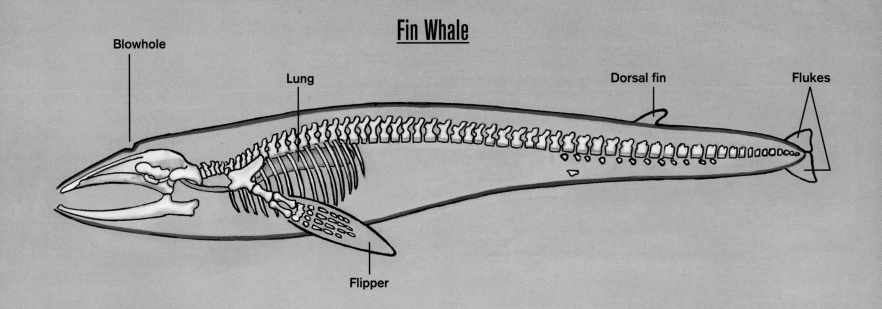

Blowhole

Lung

Dorsal fin

Flukes

Flipper

How do whales keep in touch?

With squeals, clicks, whistles, moans, barks, and other sounds. Experts listen in on whale "conversations." They hear messages going out and answers coming back. There are "Here I am" calls that seem to keep whales together. And there are "Keep away" sounds that seem to warn of danger.

Do whales have vocal cords?

No, they do not. A whale makes sounds by squeezing pouches of air near its blowhole. It is much like squeezing the bag of a bagpipe: It sets up vibrations that produce the sound.

You can make sounds the way whales do. Fill a balloon with air. Then open the neck a tiny bit. Listen to the sound the vibrations make. Of course, whales have an advantage. The vibrations inside their huge head cavities make sounds that can be heard hundreds of miles away.

Can you see a whale's ears?

No. All you can see are two tiny holes in the skin on its head. The rest of the ear is inside its head—just like human ears. But small as they are, the openings help give whales the most amazing hearing. Whales can hear sounds much higher and lower than you can. And some whales can pick up underwater sounds from as far away as 1,000 miles (1,600 km)!

Can whales see far?

Even though some whales have fairly good vision, most cannot see far under the water. Ocean waters are dark and murky. It's often impossible to see more than a few feet (meters) ahead. Experts think that whales spy-hop, or poke their heads out of the water, to take a look around!

How do whales find objects underwater?

Most use reflected sound, not sight. The whale makes a sound. When the sound hits an object—another whale, a fish, or a ship, for example—it echoes back. If the echo comes back quickly, the whale knows the object is close. If it takes longer, the object is farther away.

Finding objects by reflected sound is called echolocation. It lets whales "see" with their ears, just as you see with your eyes.

Are whales smart?

Scientists think so. Most whales work well with others of their kind. They form circles to fight off enemy whales. They come to the aid of cows that are giving birth. Sometimes a male whale, called a bull, helps a cow care for her calf.

Brain size is one way scientists measure intelligence. Sperm whales, for example, have the biggest brain of any animal in that size range. This whale's brain can weigh up to 43 pounds (19.4 kg)—about 15 times as much as the human brain!

Whale

Do whales swim like fish?

No. Whales have two big, flat back fins, called flukes. The flukes are horizontal. Beating the flukes up and down pushes the whales forward in the water. Their two flippers, which are like paddles, help them turn, dive, and roll.

Fish tails are different. They are up and down, or vertical. Fish swim by moving their tails from side to side.

How fast do whales swim?

Most whales cruise along at speeds of 3 to 5 miles (5 to 8 km) an hour. The fastest ones can surge up to 35 miles (56 km) an hour.

What keeps whales warm?

Very thick skin and lots of blubber. The skin of one very large kind of whale, the sperm whale, measures 14 inches (35.5 cm)—the thickest of any animal. Its blubber, the fatty layer under the skin, is 1 to 2 feet (30 to 60 cm) thick. No need for a heavy coat of fur to keep these animals warm!

Fish

Where do whales live?

In all the oceans of the world. Some stay in the icy cold waters near the North and South Poles all year long. Others never leave the warm tropical seas. And some move around a little to find food. But a few kinds migrate, or move from place to place.

Whales that migrate travel twice a year—in the spring and in the fall. These journeys are some of the longest of any animal. Each migration may cover thousands of miles (kilometers) and take a few months.

Why do whales migrate?

Mostly to find food. In the spring, migrating whales head to the polar regions. Here the sun shines 24 hours a day, and the cold waters bubble with life. The hungry whales find plenty to eat. They gain a lot of weight and develop a thick layer of blubber. The blubber gives migrating whales a storehouse of food.

Before the polar waters freeze over, migrating whales head back to warmer waters. Here the whales mostly rest. Pregnant cows give birth to calves. When the calves are a few months old, it is time for the whales to return to the cold, food-rich waters.

Do migrating whales travel alone or in groups?

Some travel alone; others travel in groups, called pods. Each pod has between three and hundreds of whales.

Day and night the pod swims slowly through the water, hardly ever stopping. Although the distances are great, the whales stick together. In case of trouble, they help each other. Whales have been known to lift a wounded companion with their heads. By keeping an injured whale's blowhole out of the water, they can save it from drowning!

What do whales drink?

Whales cannot drink seawater any more than you can. That's because whales' blood is less salty than seawater. If a whale drinks seawater, its tissues give up water to dilute the salt. As water gets drawn off, the whale gets very thirsty—and might die.

Experts think whales are like camels. They get all the water they need by burning fat. Whales' fatty diet and stores of blubber make drinking water unnecessary.

Do whales sleep?

Not the way you do. Whales just nap on the surface for a few minutes at a time. That's because whales have to think about breathing. It's not automatic as it is in humans.

A whale sometimes appears to sleep. But a part of its brain is always awake. Some say the brain remains awake to remind the whale to breathe!

Are whales dangerous?

Not usually. Whales are very gentle creatures. But it can be dangerous to feed, pet, or tease a whale in the wild. And don't get between a mother whale and her calf! Whales rush to attack if they think a calf is in trouble.

Wounded whales sometimes cause trouble. They may come up beneath a small boat and tip it over. Or they may slap the water with their flukes, sending huge amounts of water into a boat.

How long do most whales live?

From 15 to 60 years. The largest whales can live longer—up to 100 years. But sad to say, few whales reach old age. Life is difficult in the wild.

Some whales are killed by other whales; others starve to death or die of disease. Chemical pollution of the ocean waters and noise pollution shorten the lives of far too many whales.

TOOTHED WHALES

Do all whales have teeth?

Nearly nine out of ten kinds of whales do. They are called toothed whales. Most toothed whales have from 2 to more than 50 teeth at some time in their life. Some toothed whales have over 200 teeth!

All toothed whales are the same in another way. They have a single blowhole. The other whales have double blowholes.

Do toothed whales chew their food?

No. Toothed whales use their teeth for catching prey or tearing apart large pieces of prey. But their teeth are not for chewing. They swallow their food whole and often alive. Young whales that have no teeth, or whales with few teeth, trap prey in their jaws and suck them in.

Toothed whales feed on many kinds of fish, including squid. Squid are usually about the size of a cucumber. But the giant squid can be 50 feet (15 m) long—about half the length of a basketball court!

How big are whale teeth?

As long as 10 inches (25 cm) and can weigh more than half a pound (0.2 kg) in most whales! That's longer, and far heavier, than a dinner knife. Imagine brushing a mouth full of teeth like that twice a day!

Which is the largest of the toothed whales?

The sperm whale. The male is about 50 feet (15 m) long and weighs 40 tons (40.6 t). It is much larger than the female, which is 36 feet (11 m) and 22 tons (22.4 t). From 30 to 60 extremely large teeth line the lower jaw of an adult sperm whale.

You can tell a sperm whale by the huge square head that makes up more than a third of its body. Remember, if you spot a floating mountain, it may be a sperm whale!

What do sperm whales eat?

Mostly squid and fish that live at the bottom of the sea. To catch them, the sperm whale dives straight down. Its streamlined body slices through the water like a sleek submarine.

   Each sperm whale nabs as many squid as possible. Often the long-bodied, wiggly creatures fight back. The whale must struggle to swallow them. Scars inside the stomachs of sperm whales show that the squid keep on battling—even when the chase is over.

How long can a sperm whale hold its breath?

Between 1 and 2 hours. That time span is longer than that of most other kinds of whales. A sperm whale can also dive deeper than any other whale. One sperm whale was tracked down 7,380 feet (2,214 m). That's almost 1.5 miles (2.4 km), the height of five Empire State Buildings stacked on top of each other!

Which is the world's most famous sperm whale?

Moby Dick. The book by that name was written by Herman Melville in 1851. It tells the exciting story of a great white sperm whale that Captain Ahab longs to kill because the whale once bit off his leg. The captain battles Moby Dick but eventually loses everything— including his life.

Why did whalers hunt the sperm whale?

Mostly for the oil in its body. The bulk of this whale's huge head is filled with two kinds of oil—sperm oil and spermaceti. People burned sperm oil in lamps before the invention of electric lights. And workers in factories used this oil to grease machines. Candlemakers used spermaceti to make candles. Whalers also boiled down blubber to get more oil.

Which whale has the longest tooth?

The male narwhal. Its one tooth, or tusk, is up to 10 feet (3 m) long. Sharp and twisted, the tusk juts straight out of its mouth. It used to remind people of the unicorn, an imaginary horselike animal with one horn. In fact, narwhal tusks were once sold as unicorn horns!

Of what use is the tusk?

No one knows for sure. Narwhals sometimes seem to use their tusks as spears for catching large fish. Other times, they seem to use their tusks as ice picks. Or they may use them as tools for digging fish, squid, and shellfish out of the muddy ocean bottom.

Many scientists now think the tusk is mainly used for fighting during mating season. One reason is that many adult males have scars on their heads. Another is that many old males have broken tusks.

How did narwhals get their name?

From the Norwegian word *narhval*, meaning "corpse whale." Narwhals really do look like they are dead. They are dull gray in color, have puffy, swollen bodies, and often swim belly up.

Where are narwhals found?

Only in Arctic waters. Narwhals live in deep water close to ice. They seem to follow the ice as it breaks up and drifts away.

Narwhals move toward shore in summer when the ice starts to melt. They migrate in the fall when the ice starts to build up. Sad to say, many narwhals get trapped by fast-forming ice, and die.

Which whale is called "sea canary"?

The beluga whale. The beluga sometimes sings or trills like a songbird when it comes up to breathe. But unlike any canary you may know, it also whistles, clicks, growls, and moos. In Russia, a very loud person is said to "squeal like a beluga."

The beluga has a very high, rounded forehead called a melon. The melon helps the whale send and receive sounds. But when it wants to break through ice it uses its back, not its melon. Ouch!

Why does the beluga snap its jaws together?

No one knows. Experts think belugas may do this to scare away their enemies or to warn away other belugas. The sound of its slamming jaws can be loud and frightening.

At times, the beluga opens its jaws very wide. That's another mystery. The beluga doesn't use its teeth to catch or hold prey. Could it be that it shows its teeth to warn foes? The sight of an open mouth with as many as 40 teeth is alarming, indeed!

What do belugas fear most of all?

Polar bears. In Arctic waters, the belugas swim under blocks of ice. From time to time they come up for a breath of air. Often, a polar bear waits near an opening in the ice. As the beluga's blowhole appears, the bear strikes the whale with a powerful blow to the head. This knocks the beluga senseless—and provides a dinner for the bear.

Which is the most common toothed whale?

Most likely the dolphin, which is a kind of small whale. Each dolphin has between 100 and 200 teeth. Many have skin-covered beaks with teeth. Teeth and beaks are perfect for eating fish, squid, and different kinds of shellfish.

Why do dolphins whistle?

To keep in touch with other dolphins. Whistling is a form of communication. Each dolphin has its own sound, a "signature whistle" that other members of its group recognize.

   The whistles of male dolphins sound much like their mothers' whistles. Females end up with their own special sounds. Sometimes dolphins copy whistles of other dolphins. That might be like calling a friend by his or her name.

Do dolphins live only in salt water?

Most kinds of dolphins do. But five kinds live in freshwater rivers: the Amazon River dolphin, the Chinese river dolphin, the Ganges River dolphin, the Indus River dolphin, and the franciscana. Many of these dolphins are in danger from water pollution and motor boat traffic. They also can get caught in fishing nets.

Do dolphins swim in groups?

Dolphins usually swim in large groups or herds. Each herd may have between 12 and 1,000 dolphins. The dolphins hunt for food and play together, communicating by clicks and whistles and by slapping their flukes on the surface of the water. If an animal gets sick or hurt, the others raise it up to the surface to breathe.

Can dolphins save humans?

Yes. Dolphins have been known to help humans in distress. Not long ago, a woman thrown into the sea from an exploding yacht was kept afloat by three dolphins. They moved her to a large buoy, where she waited for human help.

In May 1978, a boatload of people was lost in a thick fog off the coast of South Africa. Four dolphins nudged the boat along through dangerous water and saved many lives.

Which dolphin seems to have a smile on its face?

The bottlenose dolphin. The shape of its beak gives it a friendly, smiling look.

Bottlenose dolphins are very easy to train. A bottlenose called Flipper became the star of a TV show. You can see bottlenose dolphins in aquariums and water parks, playing baseball and jumping through hoops.

Some bottlenose dolphins are taught to do important underwater jobs. The United States Navy has taught them to look for underwater mines, to help save divers who are in trouble, and to pick up objects from the ocean bottom.

Which is the biggest dolphin?

The orca. A male orca can be up to 22 feet (7 m) long and weigh 9,900 pounds (4,450 kg). Compare this with the bottlenose, which is less than half this length and weighs no more than 400 pounds (180 kg).

The orca, sometimes called killer whale, is also one of the fastest swimming dolphins. When chasing its prey, an orca can surge up to 40 miles (64 km) an hour.

How can you spot an orca?

By its shiny black body with white undersides and the big white spot behind each eye. Orcas are easiest to see when they spy-hop, or jump straight up out of the water. They probably spy-hop to see farther.

You can also tell an orca by its 6-foot-tall (1.8 m) dorsal fin. The pointed fin sticks up out of the water as the orca swims by. The male's fin is upright and slightly forward. The female's fin is curved, more like that of a shark.

What is an orca's favorite food?

The huge tongue and lips of the giant whales. Orcas are the only whales that eat warm-blooded animals. Often hungry orcas tear a seal or walrus apart by tossing the animal in the air and playing tug-of-war. Size, speed, and 50 large, curved teeth make the orca one of the most feared hunters of the sea.

Are dolphins the same as porpoises?

No. A porpoise's snout is rounded, not pointed like a dolphin's. A dolphin also has cone-shaped teeth, while a porpoise's teeth are spade-shaped.

BALEEN WHALES

Which are the largest whales?

Baleen whales. Instead of teeth, these whales have large, stiff plates, called baleen, hanging from their upper jaws. The baleen is made of keratin, the same material as your fingernails. Each plate of baleen can be 12 feet (3.6 m) long and up to 2.5 feet (75 cm) wide. When the whale opens its mouth, you can see hundreds of baleen plates inside!

Baleen whales are generally larger than toothed whales. And, unlike their toothy cousins, baleen whales have two blowholes, not one.

What do baleen whales feed on?

Mostly krill, a kind of tiny shrimp. The rest of its food consists of fish and other sea animals, most no bigger than a pinhead.

The whale swims through the water with its huge mouth open. As much as 70 tons (71 t) of krill, water, and fish flow in at one time. The folds on the whale's throat spread apart to make room. The whale then closes its mouth and squeezes out the water with its enormous tongue. The baleen acts as a strainer, holding the krill in the whale's mouth. Gulp! What a mouthful it swallows!

How much food does a baleen whale eat in a day?

About 3 tons (3 t)! That's as much as 6,000 boxes of spaghetti!

Baleen whales that migrate feed at this rate all summer, while they are in polar waters. During this time they gain about 20 tons (20.3 t) of blubber. In the winter, they hardly eat at all. They live off the blubber they built up during the summer months.

Which is the biggest baleen whale?

The blue whale. In fact, the blue is the biggest animal that has ever lived.
Everything about the blue whale is stupendous. The blue is the length of 3 buses—100 feet
(30 m); the weight of 25 elephants—150 tons (152.4 t); and the height of a two-story
building—20 feet (6 m)! Fifty people could stand on its tongue!

   The heart of the blue whale is also impressive. The size of a small automobile, the heart
pumps 7 tons (7.1 t) of blood through the whale's body. A human could crawl through its
main artery.

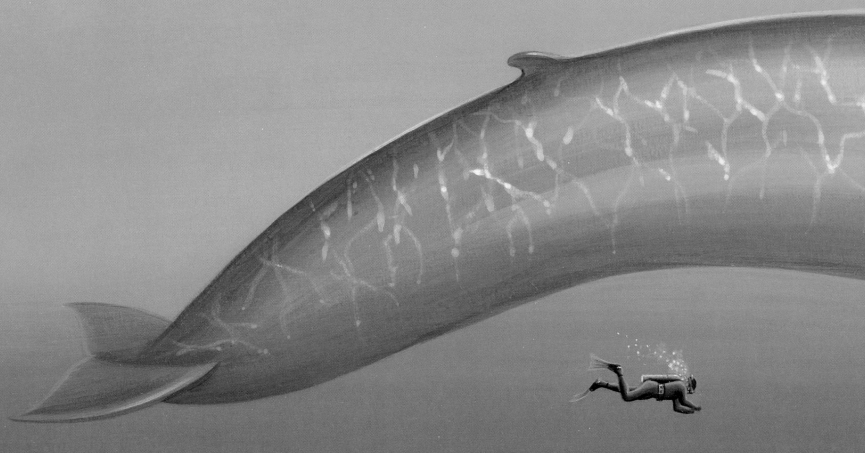

How big is a baby blue whale?

VERY! A typical newborn blue whale is about 25 feet (7.5 m) long and weighs some 2 tons (2 t). Quite a baby!

The baby blue whale nurses about 40 times a day. Each day it slurps down about 130 gallons (494 l) of its mother's rich milk. The calf gains about 10 pounds (4.5 kg) every hour. In just one week it doubles its weight! By its first birthday, a baby blue is twice as long as it was at birth.

Which is the most musical whale?

The humpback. Its "songs" consist of short groups of sounds. Each song lasts from five minutes to half an hour. And one humpback may sing the same song over and over for up to 24 hours.

A singing humpback usually stays alone about 50 feet (15 m) below the surface. Its low tones can be heard underwater as far away as 1,000 miles (1,600 km).

Why do humpbacks sing?

Nobody knows for sure. The songs may have to do with mating. Only the males, or bulls, sing. Perhaps it's their way of wooing—trying to attract female humpbacks. Or they could be telling other males to stay away.

The humpbacks seem to sing mostly in the warm waters where they mate and produce young. Humpbacks in the same breeding area sing the same song. The song seems to change from year to year. But somehow, all the singers know to make the changes.

Does the humpback whale really have a humpback?

Yes. You can see a hump in front of its dorsal fin. Also, the humpback whale actually humps, or arches, its back before it dives. And it dives very often. Every so often a humpback will jump up out of the water. This is called breaching. Then it will continue diving many times in a row. Breaching may be the humpback's way of knocking loose the half ton (0.5 t) of barnacles on its skin.

How do humpbacks catch fish?

A humpback will sometimes dive beneath a school of fish. Then it circles back up to the surface, letting out a curtain of air bubbles as it rises. The bubbles form a "net" around the small fish and move them up to the surface. The humpback then swims up, mouth wide open, and gulps down the tasty meal. One humpback whale can trap about 150 pounds (68 kg) of fish in one mouthful!

Who named the right whales?

Old-time whalers. They found these 50- to 60-foot (15 to 18 m) whales to be the "right" ones to hunt for oil and baleen.

Right whales are slow-moving, are easy to approach, and live close to shore. And since almost half of the right whale's weight is blubber, which is lighter than water, the whales float when dead. Easy to catch and land, right whales were hunted until they became few in number. Now there are fewer than 4,000 right whales left in the world's seas.

How did whalers catch right whales?

With harpoons. A whaler might shoot a harpoon into a baby right whale. The hunter knew the calf's mother would hear its baby's cries and come to help. Then the whaler would harpoon the much bigger cow.

But whalers also learned to fear right whales. The cows take very good care of their young. A cow will attack any boat that threatens her calf. Sometimes an angry mother would overturn a small whaling boat with her powerful flukes.

Do right whales "sing" like humpbacks?

No. They make low moans and high bursts of sound. But they do not sing songs like humpbacks do.

Nor can right whales take in huge mouthfuls of food like the humpbacks. Right whales do not have folds on their throats. Instead, they open and close their mouths frequently while they swim. Then, like all baleens, they scrape the food off the baleen with their tongues and swallow it.

Which whale has the longest baleen?

A bowhead. Each plate can reach 13 feet (4 m) in length. If laid end to end, the plates of one bowhead would stretch over one mile (1.6 km). The bowhead also has the thickest layer of blubber—about 2 feet (60 cm).

The bowhead takes its name from its bowed, or arched, mouth. Whalers have long hunted these whales for their oil—up to 2,835 gallons (10,773 l) in each one. By 1900, nearly all the bowheads were gone. Now they are rarely seen, and only in Arctic waters.

Which whales have the longest migration?

The gray whales. They migrate about 12,500 miles (20,000 km) a year. Each fall they leave the Arctic region and swim south along the Pacific shoreline to California and Mexico. They spend the winter there in shallow lagoons and give birth to their calves. Then, in the spring, they head back to the colder waters to eat and build up their blubber.

Do migrating grays follow a leader?

No. The first whales to head south are females about to give birth. The first group to head north are the newly pregnant females. The rest of the whales follow, swimming steadily at about 5 miles (8 km) an hour, day and night. Most likely, the migrating grays chart their course by natural landmarks along the shoreline.

Where do gray whales feed?

Often on shallow ocean bottoms. Gray whales eat a more varied diet than other baleens. In addition to fish and krill, they will eat shellfish, worms, and even plants that live on the sea floor.

To reach the food, the gray whales swim down to the mud. Usually, they roll onto their sides and scoop huge helpings of shrimp, crabs, clams, and seaweed into their mouths. Then, tilting upright, they force water out through the baleen with their tongues—and swallow what's left.

Which is the second largest whale?

The fin whale. A fin whale can be 87 feet (26 m) long. These big whales are long and narrow. Because they can swim so fast—13 miles (20 km) an hour—they are called "the greyhounds of the sea."

Fin whales are very shy. Sometimes they swim alone. If they swim in pods, the pods are made up of 10 fin whales at the most.

How did the fin whale get its name?

From the 2-foot-tall (60 cm) hooked dorsal fin that sticks up from its back.

When the fin whale surfaces, it blows a single spray about 12 to 20 feet (3.6 to 6 m) up into the air. Then the whale slowly rolls its back and fin above the water four or five times. Finally, it rises a little higher and dives down. A very deep dive, or sounding, lasts from 5 to 15 minutes.

Which is the fastest-swimming baleen whale?

Probably the sei (pronounced *say*) whale. A scientist once clocked it swimming along at an amazing 35 miles (56 km) an hour! Because it twists and turns like a small fish when swimming fast, some call it the sardine whale.

Which is the smallest baleen whale?

The pygmy right whale. These whales are usually only between 18 and 21 feet (5.4 and 6.3 m) long. Dark on top and white underneath, pygmy rights have short baleen and are found only in the Southern Hemisphere.

Will there always be whales in the seas?

That depends on all of us. The old threat to whales was from whalers. Over the years, they killed millions of whales. The new threat is from water pollution, which is shortening the lives of whales. By helping to end whaling and dumping in the seas, we can help these magnificent creatures survive into the future.

Index

About the Authors

Years ago, the Bergers took their first whale-watching cruise and got hooked on writing about whales and dolphins. Since then, they've shared their excitement about these marvelous mammals with many readers. "To know whales is to love them," they say.

About the Illustrator

Higgins Bond was born and raised in Little Rock, Arkansas, and earned a Bachelor of Fine Arts degree at the Memphis College of Art. She has worked for more than twenty years as a freelance illustrator for major corporations and publishers, and she has illustrated three stamps for the United States Postal Service.